Guided

Gemma Keatley

BALBOA.
PRESS
A DIVISION OF HAY HOUSE

Balboa Press books may be ordered through booksellers or by contacting:

Balboa Press
A Division of Hay House
1663 Liberty Drive
Bloomington, IN 47403
www.balboapress.com.au
1 (877) 407-4847

Because of the dynamic nature of the Internet, any web addresses or links contained in this book may have changed since publication and may no longer be valid. The views expressed in this work are solely those of the author and do not necessarily reflect the views of the publisher, and the publisher hereby disclaims any responsibility for them.

The author of this book does not dispense medical advice or prescribe the use of any technique as a form of treatment for physical, emotional, or medical problems without the advice of a physician, either directly or indirectly. The intent of the author is only to offer information of a general nature to help you in your quest for emotional and spiritual well-being. In the event you use any of the information in this book for yourself, which is your constitutional right, the author and the publisher assume no responsibility for your actions.

Any people depicted in stock imagery provided by Thinkstock are models, and such images are being used for illustrative purposes only.
Certain stock imagery © Thinkstock.

Printed in the United States of America.

ISBN: 978-1-4525-1333-1 (sc)
ISBN: 978-1-4525-1334-8 (e)

Balboa Press rev. date: 2/21/2014

Contents

Chapter 1

A Story

I was young, a girl of maybe ten or eleven, when the soldiers came, and it's funny now that I think back to those days, I can only remember them through the eyes of a child.

But where do I start? Well, I suppose with the most important part.

I remember my mother, with her coppery red hair and slight frame, always working hard on the farm. I remember my father, big and strong, working out in the field. Looking back now, I find it strange that I was not blessed with brothers and sisters, but I think it was not for lack of trying. I remember a plot of garden with several wooden crosses lovingly laid with flowers.

Sometimes in the evening, I would sneak a peek out of the window and see my mother crying in the garden. She would compose herself before her return, but when she tucked me in at night and kissed me so gently, I could feel that her face was still wet.

One night, my mother called me to her, and we sat in front of the hearth. She pulled me up on her lap and told me a story. She said that all would be well because I was not "Jewish," but that some soldiers were coming and it was best that we were away when they arrived. She told me not to worry, but her brow was furrowed.

I asked where my father was, and she said he was seeing a man about a secure passage. I had no idea what any of these things were, but some of the boys in the neighbouring village had started playing soldiers some time ago, and they did lots of hitting and shouting and shooting with guns, so I agreed to be a good girl and take a passage. Whatever that might involve.

The next morning, my mother woke me early. I was used to being up at daybreak to milk the cows, but this was even earlier. It felt like the middle of the night. My mother fed me the biggest breakfast I had ever seen, although it was hard to have an appetite when it was so early.

After breakfast, she carried our cases out into the laneway, and we waited. And waited. And waited.

After what seemed like ages, we saw a truck come up the laneway. It was old and rickety with a large, open truck bed at the back. As the man pulled up, I noticed the children. So many children. All ages, all sizes, and all colours, all sitting in the open air at the back of the truck.

The man apologised, said he had run into some trouble, and said that the job was going to be harder than he first thought. He pulled my mother aside, and she began to yell at the man. "You agreed!" she cried with desperation in her voice. "We've given you all we have!"

The man waited. "There's just no room," he said.

"Well, *make* room!" my mother screamed. I had never seen her so angry and upset. She stormed into the house and came out with a small package. It looked like my grandmother's old jewellery box. Out of it, she took my grandmother's pearls and her engagement ring. "Keep her safe," she said firmly to the man as she handed over our family's most precious treasures.

With that agreed upon, my mother hugged me tightly and helped me into the back of the truck.

"What about you?" I asked.

She smiled and said, "Daddy and I will meet you there very soon."

I felt uneasy, but I had never had reason to doubt her. So off I went, smiling and waving through a trail of dust.

That was the last time I ever saw my mother alive.

Chapter 2

The River

The long ride to the river was quite enjoyable. There were eighteen of us in all, crammed into a small space, and we laughed and jostled ourselves and each other as we went over the bumpy roads.

The morning air was crisp and icy, a good clue that it was going to be a glorious, sunny day. All the bustling around and the fresh air were making me suddenly hungry, and I couldn't wait to get to our destination so I could unpack the sandwiches that my mother had placed in my case earlier that day.

Around midmorning, we arrived at the riverbank. We all unloaded ourselves, and there was an air of excitement as we wondered what was next.

The man, our driver, got us to unload a wooden raft from the truck, and I giggled as I realised we had been sitting on it the whole time and had not recognised what it was. We all helped haul it from the back of the truck and into the water. One by one, we were instructed to climb on board.

It was quite a sight as we scrambled and wobbled and bobbed about. Some of us squealed when water began sloshing over the sides, and I'm sure I was not the only one with a wet bottom. Eventually, we were all aboard, with our cases all lined up neatly on the riverbank waiting to be loaded.

In the distance, down the road, we could see a trail of dust. On the other side of the river, we began to hear the bark of dogs and distant shouts. We wondered what was happening.

The man began to rush. Jumping onto the raft with several oars, he pushed it off farther into the current and yelled at the children to take the other three oars and paddle.

I stared in horror at my case, which was now getting farther and farther away. I thought of my dry clothes and my sandwiches. A moment later, however, my attention shifted to a far more serious situation.

On each side of the riverbank were soldiers. Lots of them. All in uniforms and hats, shouting at us to get out of the water. They looked furious, and their dogs were even more frightening. There were at least six dogs, drooling and snarling with a viciousness I had never encountered before.

A moment later, the men released the dogs and they charged into the water, still barking furiously and heading right for us.

Suddenly, it dawned on me that they were here for us, that there was no misunderstanding, that they did not want us out of the water because it was dangerous. They were the dangerous ones.

It was at the same moment that the little girl next to me realised the same thing, and in a frozen moment of fear, the oar she was holding slipped from her fingers and was immediately swept away.

The man was strange. He looked slowly at the girl, and he looked at the oar being sucked under the swirling water by the current. He never yelled or even spoke a word.

He glanced over at the men on the riverbanks, then at the dogs in the water, and finally back at our terrified faces. He paused and seemed to be weighing everything up.

"It's OK," he finally said, his voice expressionless. "It's all OK."

With that, he removed his white shirt and tied it carefully and deliberately around his oar and held it above his head.

Chapter 3

A Very Crowded House

The soldiers threw a rope to the man, and we were pulled ashore. We were dragged from the raft and herded up the road. Some of the unlucky ones were bitten by the dogs, and others who fell behind were hit with sticks.

We walked for miles that day. Cold, wet, hungry, tired, and sore. The older ones held hands with the younger ones and helped them along. We were forced to toilet ourselves on the side of the road in full view of everyone. It was humiliating, but for the most part, we became too tired to care.

We walked well into the afternoon. We walked as the sun set, and we walked as the moon rose. Finally, up ahead, we saw some lights.

We stumbled along until we arrived at a farmhouse, where we were permitted to wash up and eat. We had bread and soup, and though I don't remember what type of soup it was, it was the best that I had ever tasted.

The fire warmed my aching bones, and as we were sent to bed with six children in each—three at the head and three at the foot—I said a silent prayer to God to thank him for delivering me to this place safely and in one piece. I closed my eyes and sank blissfully into oblivion.

Chapter 4

A New Order

We were woken early by a strong-looking, heavyset woman who seemed very matter-of-fact. She gathered us into the kitchen where large loaves of fresh bread were sitting on the table still steaming.

She looked us all in the eye and told us that we were in her house now, which meant following her rules. There would be roll call in the morning and roll call in the evening. If anyone was missing, all would go hungry until the missing child was found. We would work and we would work hard, and there would be no complaining. Anyone caught stealing, fighting, or generally misbehaving would be whipped.

She finished her little speech with, "Is that understood?"

After we had all offered up a chorus of, "Yes, missus," she seemed quite pleased with herself and maybe even a little surprised that it had gone so well. She wiped her hands on her apron and said, "Right then, let's eat."

And so began our life in the crowded house.

The woman never explained who she was, or whose side she was on, and I had a very hard time trying to work out who the enemy actually was and what was really going on.

I decided that the enemy was someone who treated you badly and hurt you, and this woman didn't seem to be doing either. So I moved her out of the enemy category and put her in the boss category as someone to be minded.

The soldiers from the raft I was also unsure about. They were frightening and they did set their dogs on us and hit us with sticks, but overall, I'm not sure that they were enemies either. This whole war business seemed very complicated to me.

My days in the crowded house were long and happy. We all missed home and still had no word as to what was happening in the world and what it meant for us. But we soon settled into a routine and a rhythm. Life, as it so often does, just became a new kind of normal.

In the mornings (and again in the afternoons), it was my job to milk the cow. She was a beautiful thing. Placid and friendly, it always surprised me how she alone managed to produce enough milk for the woman and eighteen hungry children. I used to talk with her often about my day, about life before the crowded house, and about my hopes and dreams of the future, for when I got back home to my mother and father.

She didn't talk back much, but she would occasionally give a bit of a moo, which I interpreted as an amen to what I had been saying.

After breakfast, it was my job to supervise the younger ones and help them to do their chores. We cleaned and we scrubbed. We aired out the beds, and we washed all the sheets by hand and hung them out to dry. We swept and we polished, and when we were done, we started on the lunch.

The little ones looked up to me, I think, and I had a real soft spot for each of them. They knew that I could be counted on to kiss a sore bit better or offer a kind word. I didn't yell and curse at them as much as some of the older children did, and I think they found some small comfort in this.

The days were busy, and there never seemed to be a moment to rest. However, in the afternoons, I was lucky. It was my job to gather wood for the fire. The boys did all the hard chopping, but I was allowed to wander off and collect kindling each day. Maybe the woman saw some value in my work in keeping the household running, so she granted me this reprieve each afternoon.

After my afternoon kindling expeditions, it was back to milk the cow again and to help the little ones prepare the dinner. This was a lively time full of excited chatter about the day and usually how good it was to have something to eat.

It was in the evenings though that the children raised their fears. As we huddled together in our beds, some would whimper quietly and others would talk about what-if. What if we never get home? What if the soldiers come for us again? What if …? In order to calm their fears, I would tell them stories, always something funny or with a happy ending, and I would help them to say their prayers.

I would tell them that the prayers of children are stronger than any other and that God always answers the prayers of children first. Then we would all, the older children included, put our prayers together, to make them super strong.

We all slept soundly after that.

Chapter 5

Berries

One afternoon, I was out gathering twigs when I spied in the distance what looked like a berry patch. It was quite a distance away through the trees, so I couldn't be sure. I usually foraged much closer to the farmhouse, but today the sun was shining and the air was delicious and warm. I thought of how exciting it would be to return home with enough juicy berries to feed us all, and my mind was made up.

I was so excited that I had been right about the berry patch that I was soon lost in the task of picking. I had eaten until my stomach was near bursting, and I now had an apron overflowing with them.

I wiped the sweat from my brow and sat on the cool grass under the shade of a nearby tree to rest. I began to wonder where we would have ended up if the soldiers hadn't come and our little raft had been allowed to float unhindered to our destination. It seemed to me that we had ended up in a place that seemed safe enough. The rules and consequences were clear and everybody had their part to play. The woman was kind to us, and it was so lovely to be surrounded with children and their laughter.

Little did I realise it was all about to change.

Chapter 6

A Dream

I must have drifted off to sleep because the surroundings suddenly looked different. Lighter and shimmering. A woman appeared before me, and I stared in wonder as I realised that it was my mother. She looked radiant—healthy and strong, her coppery hair shining in the sunlight. Around her neck, she wore my grandmother's pearls, and on her finger was her engagement ring.

"Darling, you must listen to me now. I'm going to tell you a story," she said.

"OK," I murmured.

"You must not go back to the crowded house. It is no longer safe. You must go instead to the highest hill to where the abbey sits. Listen for the bells. You must tell them that an angel has sent you and that you are to do God's work within the abbey's walls."

"Do you understand me? You will be safe then."

"OK," I murmured again, sleepily.

"I love you," she whispered. And then, just as magically as she had arrived, she was gone.

I awoke with a start and looked around to see where she could have gone. She left me with such a feeling of peace and calm, even though the words she spoke were disturbing.

As a child, I had sometimes had visions of angels who would tell me things, but I usually dismissed them as being fanciful imagination. This vision had been so vivid and real though, and it made me realise just how much I missed home.

I gathered up the berries that had fallen out of my apron and began to walk back to the crowded house, wanting to hear what the children would think of my mother's warning.

I was just approaching the clearing when I heard a gunshot ring out. It cracked through the air so loudly that I was momentarily deafened. I began to run towards that house but stopped dead in my tracks as I saw a scene of horror before me.

Out the front of the house were soldiers. They had no dogs this time, but they didn't need them. The children were lined up against the wall of the farmhouse. The woman was pleading and arguing and yelling at the men, and on the ground in a pool of blood was our cow.

I just stood there frozen with my mouth open. At first, I couldn't make sense of anything. Our cow? Why would anyone want to hurt our cow? That's when I saw the trucks. They had come for the children. They had come to take the children and the woman wouldn't let them. So they took something else. In that moment, I knew who the enemy was.

The woman screamed, and a soldier hit her hard across the face. Even from a distance hiding behind the trees, I heard the crack, and she fell lifeless to the ground. She did not move.

The soldiers pointed their guns at the children. At *my* children. They hit them and poked them with their guns, and they forced them into the trucks.

All I could do was watch, paralysed and completely helpless, as the enemy took my family away.

When the last of the trucks had left, I crumpled to the ground, daring to breathe for the first time. Tears streamed down my face as I contemplated what had just happened. The woman was still not moving, and neither was my beautiful cow.

The life that I had known was now over, and as I prayed to God for help, my mother's voice came back loud and clear. "Go to the highest hill where the abbey sits. Listen for the bells."

What bells? I called out in my mind, and that's when I heard them. Very faintly, I heard them pealing. It may have been my imagination, but it was enough. I turned in the opposite direction of the crowded house. With just me and my berries, I started to walk.

Chapter 7

A New Direction

The first night was the worst. I was completely unprepared for outdoor living. I had dressed lightly when I set off to collect the berries, and I had been too terrified to go back to the crowded house to pack anything for my journey. At least the weather had been mild.

I walked as far and as fast as I could in the moonlight, and then I slept under the cover of trees until the day's break.

The next day, I came across another farmhouse that was abandoned. I could only assume that the soldiers had not just come for us but for others as well. Their poor cow remained unmilked, and their chickens were raucously squawking for food.

I guess I knew the dangers, but I chose to ignore them. I got to work milking the cow and then found some chicken feed to sort out the chickens. I entered the farmhouse where there was still food set on the table. It looked as though the soldiers had taken everyone by surprise.

I was starving, so I helped myself to the fresh milk and the leftovers at the table. And then, God forgive me, I took a heavy winter coat, a water flask, and some additional food.

I was careful not to disturb anything else, and I didn't linger as my fear got the better of me and I imagined soldiers approaching from every direction. Suddenly, I heard a noise and I sprinted away from the farmhouse like a startled rabbit.

I'm sure it was just my imagination, or maybe just the cow kicking over the empty bucket I had left out in the paddock. But it was enough to remind me to avoid other farms from now on.

After calming my nerves with a few deep breaths and a good talking to, I continued on my way with far more confidence now that I was warm and fed. I was surprised at myself that I still had the energy to walk despite my lack of sleep. I had no idea at the time that it was just my good friend adrenalin doing me a favour.

I'm sure I thought about lots of things on that journey, but mostly I just walked. Had I been older or understood more about the real dangers that faced me, I would have probably been more scared, but as luck would have it, I didn't understand these things. So I got on with it and just kept putting one foot in front of the other.

Being in nature was calming for me, and though I was alone, it was still noisy. There were rushing creeks to cross and birds screeching above and around me. There were rustling trees and a strong and sometimes deafening wind that swept in several times each day. And of course, there was me, huffing and puffing as I stomped along clumsily, heart pounding wildly when I tripped over a fallen branch, got tangled in brambles, or just lost my footing on the uneven ground.

My favourite and most comforting sounds were the bells. They did not come like clockwork, but I could generally hear them in the morning and in the afternoon. They became my companions, like a beacon calling me forward, encouraging and directing me, and reminding me that there was a safe place waiting for me, maybe even around the next corner.

Chapter 8

The Abbey

After many, many gruelling days of walking, I finally saw it. The abbey that I had been seeking was at the top of a nearby hill. The bells rang loudly that morning, and in my excitement, I picked up my pace, determined to reach the abbey by midday.

I was possibly a little ambitious, as it was just on sunset when I arrived on the doorstep.

Suddenly, a great fear gripped me. What if there was no one here? What if the soldiers had arrived here before me? What if they didn't believe what my mother had told me to say? What if they sent me away?

I thought of my children in the crowded house. I said to myself out loud, "The prayers of children are stronger than any other, and God always answers the prayers of children first."

I knocked on the solid wooden doors. And then I dropped to my knees and began to pray.

Chapter 9

Mother Superior

When the door was finally opened by a sister in a full nun's habit, I was still kneeling, my hands clasped together. I gazed up at her up with a look of immense relief, hope, and gratitude. She just looked confused and shocked.

I don't know how I had been expecting her to react. I guess in my fantasies I had imagined that they were expecting me and would embrace me like a long-lost daughter. In hindsight, considering the state of me, and the grime that I must have been coated in, confused and shocked were probably not so bad.

The sister brought me in out of the cold and not too gruffly asked me to explain myself. As my mother had instructed, I told her that an angel had sent me and that I was to do God's work within the abbey.

"Well, not looking like *that* you won't," she scolded me gently. "Come on then. Let's get you washed up and see what's really hiding under all that grot."

With that, I was led to a freezing room where she scrubbed me from head to toe with soap, cold water, and a washer. She put me in a very plain white cotton nightdress that was way too long in every possible sense. Then she took me to the kitchen and sat me down to a bowl of hot broth and dry bread.

Apart from my initial greeting, if you could call it that, she never said another word, just pointed to where she wanted me to go and handed me things. It didn't feel rude, just strange, and I knew better than to speak without being spoken too. So I stayed silent.

When she left the room, I ate ravenously until every crumb and every drop of broth was finished. I was embarrassed at my lack of manners but so relieved to finally have something hot in my belly. I hungrily looked around for more, but I didn't dare try to help myself to seconds.

As the bread and broth slowly filled me and the hunger pangs subsided, I cautiously began to look around. Apart from a large preparation bench, a stove, and a fireplace with a large cooking pot, the large room seemed empty.

The fireplace had burned down to just a few coals and ash, and the light from the lantern she had left with me flickered unpredictably, threatening at any moment to go out. The place felt cold and dark, and the eerie silence was making me nervous. Everything about the place seemed foreign to me, and I wondered why on earth my mother would send me here.

Eventually, the sister returned to collect me and took me to an office. At least this space was well lit and warm, thanks to an open fire.

I was enjoying feeling warm for the first time in a long time when another woman in full nun's habit entered the room. She was tall and slim and looked very old. If you had asked me quietly, I would have said she looked about one hundred, but looking back, I'm sure she would have only been in her late forties or early fifties. She walked confidently and with purpose, and her face looked kind.

She motioned for me to sit down and asked me to tell my story.

"But how on God's green earth did you *find* us?" she asked.

"The bells led me here. Twice a day, the bells would ring, and I just followed them," I replied.

For a moment, she didn't respond. Her brow was furrowed and she seemed to be thinking hard on something. When she spoke, her words were slow and careful and considered. "But the bells have not been rung here for over thirty years."

She looked to the heavens, made the sign of the cross with her hands, and quietly said a prayer, which I could not hear.

She took my hands in hers and looked deeply into my eyes. She said, "God welcomes you here, my child. You will be safe here."

Unfortunately, I was about to discover that safe and happy were two different things, and having one does not necessarily guarantee the other.

Chapter 10

A Rude Awakening

Some of the sisters were kind to me. They spoke with me of my home and understood that I was missing my family. They understood that I needed a place to call home.

The others were not so understanding. They believed that the abbey was no place for children and that I would be a disruption. They believed that children carried sin and needed discipline. They wanted me to live at the orphanage down the hill and learn my place in the world. They said that if it was God's will that the soldiers take me, then so be it.

I was assigned chores around the abbey, but the sisters complained that I was not pulling my weight. They complained that I was too slow and that I disrupted their devotionals purely by being present. Some often knocked over my water bucket when I was scrubbing the floors and knocked dishes out of my hands when I was clearing the table, saying things like, "Oh, I'm sorry I didn't see you there. I wasn't expecting a child to be in the abbey."

It was hard to be despised for something that I could not help, and as a result, I became masterful at being invisible and keeping out of people's way.

The only one who seemed to truly understand me was Mother Superior. She spent the time getting to know me, and I got the feeling that I was in some way an answer to one of her prayers.

The angels continued to visit me often in the abbey, sometimes even daily. They spoke to me with great wisdom on things that I did not understand. Mother Superior, however, was a wise woman herself, and she implored me to write of what I had heard.

I told her that I had not learned to read or write, so she began to teach me. She was a woman who took God's word seriously, and as she was asked to keep me safe and help me do God's work within the abbey walls, she would not send me to the convent school at the bottom of the hill with the other children. The other sisters were angry at the attention which I received.

Mother had me begin by copying large sections of sacred texts, and gradually I began to understand how each letter could be sounded out to make a word. Although I learned very quickly how to write, my reading and understanding were not as good. And the texts were so complex that in the end, I gave up trying to understand what was being said and instead focussed mainly on carefully copying the words that my angels spoke.

Mother would often ask me about things, and the words that I spoke were not my own. This seemed to come naturally to me, so I was not bothered by it.

I began to settle into my life at the abbey and to feel that I was making a contribution. Slowly, but surely, the other sisters began to accept my presence and life became much more tolerable.

I was around seventeen when peace was finally declared and those who were still able began returning to their homes. On my eighteenth birthday, Mother Superior called me to her and asked me if I wished to return home to my family.

I felt torn as I was so grateful for the life that she had provided me, but I was desperate for news of my parents. So she arranged for a horse and driver to take me home, with the promise that if all was not as I expected, then I was to return to her immediately.

Chapter 11

Home

The journey home was much faster by way of a horse, but even still, it took two full days riding. I stopped in a village and was offered prearranged lodging with a woman and her six children in a farmhouse. It was so lovely to be welcomed by people who were real and genuine. The war had taken a toll on everyone in some way. The woman I stayed with had lost her husband and most of her possessions had been looted. She had hidden with friends until the war had ended and was starting to rebuild her life. We talked into the early hours of the morning, and it was good.

The next afternoon, I arrived back in my village and the driver took me up the lane to my home. I remembered back to the day I had so naively waved my mother off, never realising how dramatically my life was about to change. I was older now and different, but I really did expect my mother and father to come running out to greet me. Instead, I was greeted with a whole lot of nothing.

The farmhouse was empty. Completely empty. The windows were all broken and the roof had partially fallen in. The animals were gone, as was everything of value in the sheds.

As I was surveying the scene, the local minister, who had heard of my arrival, came to greet me. I embraced him warmly, glad to finally, after all these years, see a familiar face. And it warmed my heart that he remembered me.

"I'm so, so sorry," he said. I thought he was talking about the state of the farm. "It's OK," I said. "We can fix it up." He looked at me awkwardly and with sympathy, and that's when I knew that he was not talking about the farm.

"Oh. All right," I said as the numbness engulfed me. I didn't know what else to say. We stood in silence, both unsure what to say next. I couldn't bring myself to ask the details, so I just stood there.

He offered me lodging with himself and his wife, which I gratefully accepted. It was close to sunset so he said, "Take your time and I will wait for you." He walked away to give me space.

I went into the garden, where the crosses of my brothers and sisters lay. There were now two additional crosses carefully positioned next to them. I pulled away the weeds and overgrowth and lovingly laid some fresh wild flowers on them. And then, just as my mother had done all those years ago, I fell to my knees and wept.

I sobbed for what felt like an eternity. I cried for the good things and for the bad. I cried for my parents and for the brothers and sisters I never met. I cried for the man on the raft and for the children of the crowded house. I cried for the woman and her cow. I cried for the sandwiches that I never got to eat and for the time I was really little and I dropped the eggs whilst I was collecting them. I cried until there was nothing left to cry for.

And then, just as my mother had done, I picked myself up and composed myself. Once again, I put one foot in front of the other.

Chapter 12

A New Home

The next morning, I thanked the minister for his generosity and asked him to arrange the sale of my family farm. I asked him to keep half of the takings for his ministry on the condition that he maintain the memorial plot of my garden. I asked that the rest of the money be directed to Mother Superior at the abbey, where I would now be taking my vows.

Mother Superior welcomed me home with open arms and even tears. It felt good to belong. I asked permission to take my vows, and she readily accepted me. It took three long years, but I became an official sister and a bride of Christ.

With my newfound commitment to the abbey, the other sisters began to respect me. They welcomed me cautiously into their philosophical discussions and were less inclined to bully. There were still a few who refused to welcome me and still referred to me as the "Devil's disruption."

My work with Mother continued, and by that time, I had written volumes on all aspects of morality, social justice, and religious integrity.

I still had very little understanding of what it all meant, but it seemed to be of value so I kept writing.

I became so used to speaking to my angels for Mother that I was totally taken by surprise when one day I received an unusual message all of my own.

My own mother visited me again in a dream and said, "My darling, I want to tell you a story."

I listened in wonder and amazement as my mother told me that not all was lost and that I was going to be blessed with a child. This child would be my own, and I was to love and care for her and to protect her always.

I was left conflicted and reeling from this. As I was an ordained sister now, I had not so much as laid eyes on a man since returning to the abbey, and I could not possibly imagine how I could bring a baby into the world.

I became terrified that I would be sent away if I revealed this information to anyone, so I kept it to myself. However, this was not serving me, and I started to lose sleep, lose weight, and became ill. After several weeks, Mother beckoned me to her and insisted that I tell her what was vexing me.

Mother listened carefully to what my mother had said and reassured me that all was well. She said that God worked in mysterious ways and that he had a plan for us all. She told me that it was not for me to worry myself about and that she would take care of it. With that, I felt the weight of the world lift off my shoulders and my health returned to me once more.

Chapter 13

A Baby

Exactly one year later, we were exiting the dining hall when there was a banging at the door. It was the same door that I had entered through on the day I arrived at the abbey.

Mother herself answered the door as the rest of us gathered, excited at the prospect of a visitor, which was indeed a very rare occurrence.

A man entered through the door flustered and full of apologies at the intrusion. I immediately recognised him as the minister of the church in my old village. In his arms, he held some old blankets. We all looked on curiously as the blankets began to move and a loud cry emerged.

The man looked visibly distressed at the screams coming from the blanket and said, "I didn't know where else to go." He pulled back the blankets to reveal a tiny infant.

There was a chorus of shocked gasps as we all began to realise what it was. "It can't stay here," one sister whispered. "It's not right to bring a child into the abbey," said another. The room erupted into judgemental tut-tuts and the noise frightened the infant. It began to cry even louder.

"Get it out of here," said one sister. "Tell it to be quiet," said another. It was clear to me that none had any understanding of babies.

I instinctively stepped forward, scooping the baby gently into my arms. I put my finger to its mouth and it began to suck hungrily. The crying stopped and the gathered crowd breathed a sigh of relief.

"She's hungry," I said, manoeuvring myself and the infant through the crowd and towards the kitchen. I warmed some cow's milk over the stove and dripped it carefully into her mouth using a basting dropper. This seemed to work well, and she drank with gusto for several minutes. Then she closed her eyes and promptly fell asleep.

Mother shooed the sisters away and spoke to the minister briefly in her office. After he left, she came to collect us from the kitchen.

"It's a baby," I said in shock and delight. "A *real* baby. How are we possibly going to look after a baby?"

"Come with me," Mother said.

She led me to a room in an area that I had never been to before. She took from her pocket a large iron key and unlocked the door.

What I saw took my breath away.

Chapter 14

A New Room

The room was beautiful. It contained a small cradle and a fine, handcrafted cot. There was a chest of drawers filled with all sizes of baby clothes and small, hand-knitted dolls and jackets. "A nursery? In the abbey?" I was utterly confused as to where this had come from or what it was for.

Mother smiled at me. "When God speaks to you, it is not for us to question but simply to answer."

I stared with admiration at the faith and wisdom that Mother had had in preparing for the arrival of this little soul.

And so it was, just as my mother had foretold, that I myself became a mother.

Chapter 15

The Most Beautiful Rose

The arrival of my baby signalled the happiest and most content time of my life. Suddenly, everything was right with the world, and I had found my reason for living.

I named her Rose, as she was perfect and beautiful yet her life had already been filled with thorns. When she arrived, she was frail and sickly. She had been severely beaten and was malnourished when the minister had found her in the bushes out the front of the village church.

For the first few weeks, it looked as though God might take her home, but she was a little fighter and never gave up.

Of course, the other sisters were furious that she had been allowed to stay and that I had been allocated to care for her. They began to call her "the Devil's child" sent to destroy the peace of the abbey and introduce temptation and unholy desires into the order.

Mother declared that Rose's arrival was the will of God and that they were not to interfere in this. The sisters kept quiet but began to plot.

Chapter 16

School

When Rose turned six, the sisters insisted that she be properly educated in the convent school where some of them taught. This meant that Rose would be sent away to live with other orphans down the bottom of the hill near the village.

I argued that to separate her from the only family that she had known was not right, but the sisters persisted until Mother relented and she was sent away. Mother calmed my fears by giving me permission to visit each fortnight and by saying that Rose would benefit from mixing with the other children.

After a month at the school, it was clear that all was not well with Rose. She became quiet and withdrawn and stopped speaking. The smile was gone from her face, and it was breaking my heart.

When I was permitted to visit her, I pulled her into a close embrace; she flinched and pulled away. This was not the affectionate girl that I had known. I asked her gently to show me the cuts, welts, and bruises that now covered most of her body.

In a rage, I stormed into the teacher's office and the sister just smirked at me. "She is the Devil's child and she needs to be punished." She declared, "Discipline is the only thing that will save her from her sins."

I was furious. I went to Mother and demanded that she be removed from the school. Mother had a better plan.

Chapter 17

A Teacher

On Monday morning, I began my teaching career. I was assigned to teach Rose's class, which consisted of eight children. I taught them to read, write, and count, and all aspects of religious education. We sang songs and played learning games, and although I was initially doubtful of my abilities, after a few weeks of settling in, I felt completely at ease. Some of the other teachers were wonderful, and I made some firm friends.

Rose began to flourish again, and because her classes with a certain teacher were limited, the bruises faded, never to return.

I thoroughly enjoyed my years of teaching and writing, and my skills were put to use in designing new curriculum and implementing more positive discipline practices.

I loved all the children dearly and I had a sense of pride as they grew and developed into healthy, happy, young adults.

Rose was well liked by all the other children and grew used to living in the company of others. I still felt guilty that I couldn't be with her at night, but I imagined that she felt comforted by the presence of the others in her own little crowded house.

Chapter 18

Big Changes

When Rose was twelve years old, God called Mother Superior home. It was all very sudden, and even my angels gave me no forewarning. It was a devastating blow to me as she had been a mentor, a protector, and as time went on, a friend. I was honoured to know her, and though I knew she was with God, the grief was intense.

The abbey was in mourning for a whole month, and then I was both devastated and horrified to learn that the sister who had beaten my little Rose at school was to be appointed as our new Mother Superior. She still condemned me for my arrival at the abbey and still considered Rose to be spawn of the Devil.

She had all of my writings destroyed, and she called me to her new office and informed me that I had no authority to speak with God or angels and that it was all nonsense. She told me that it was the Devil that had been speaking through me and that because Christ valued forgiveness, I would be forgiven if I never did it or spoke of it again.

She told me that she had found Rose a Job in another village. It was customary for the orphans to leave the orphanage at sixteen to seek work, but Rose was still a child. I stated my concerns but was chastised for questioning her authority.

On the eve of her thirteenth birthday, my little girl was sent out into the world, and my world fell apart.

Chapter 19

Deeper and Deeper

I threw myself into my work with the other orphans, hoping to numb the pain, until new Mother decided that it was time for a change and reassigned me from teaching to garden work. This was something that I had never enjoyed and something that felt very unnatural to me. The work was physically demanding, and my aging joints suffered as a result.

Rose and I had promised to write to each other, and we did so every week. The letters were my only link to what was good in my life.

When new Mother discovered the letters, she insisted that letter writing was not an appropriate pastime and that I needed to devote myself to more godly duties. She assigned me to the vigil or prayer time in the chapel between twelve midnight and 4:00 a.m. each night, on my own, in addition to my daily work. This was normally something that we all shared on a roster.

Despite her ruling, I continued to write to Rose in secret every week. But then her letters stopped coming. I wrote asking if all was well and received no reply. I understood that she had her own life now and was probably too busy to reply, but still I worried dreadfully about her.

I approached new Mother and asked for leave to visit Rose. I was told that it was not possible and to forget about her. "Rose is no longer your concern, and it is not right for you to be so attached," she replied coldly.

She told me that perhaps my mind would be better served in the kitchen. So after a 5:30 a.m. start with prayers and devotionals, I would head out for a full day of weeding, digging, planting, and harvesting. It was then my task to take the day's harvest and scrub, rinse, peel, and chop the vegetables for us all, in preparation for each night's meal.

I would eat with the others and attend evening prayers before retiring to bed in order to arise at 11:45 p.m. to attend midnight vigil. I got back into bed at 4:15 a.m. and then rose again at 5:30 a.m. to repeat the process over and over, seven days a week.

By this stage, even the other sisters were feeling sorry for me and would pass sympathetic glances my way in the hallways. Some offered to share the midnight vigil with me, but they were chastised and forbidden to do it.

When winter came and the snow began to fall, the other sisters were brought indoors for assignment to indoor tasks, but my reassignment never came.

The ice burned my skin and scorched my lungs, my joints were swollen and painful, and by the end of each day, I could hardly hold the knife to chop the vegetables. I began to cook them without peeling them and was publicly chastised for sloppy workmanship.

I was still young, but my body had begun to shut down on me. By the next winter, I finally gave in and my body collapsed.

Chapter 20

A Better Life

The sisters carried me in from the snow and placed me in my bed. The fever started and I began to dream.

I dreamt of a new life, a better life, a life free from physical and emotional pain. I dreamt of a world where I still had a mother and a father. A world where there was no war. I imagined a life with living brothers and sisters who loved each other and looked after each other, and where no one was separated by distance or circumstance. I began to dream of a life in which I was permitted to love and maybe even find a husband of my own. Someone who would love me deeply and who would nurture and protect me. And I dreamt of having children of my very own. Children that I would love with all of my heart.

I dreamt of a world in which I could speak freely with my angels without censure or ridicule, and I dreamt of Rose.

I knew that all of these things were impossible and too much to ask. I knew that I no longer had the strength of a child's prayer, but the child inside me prayed with everything I had that God might hear me and take me to a better life.

Chapter 21

My Beautiful Bells

As I lay on the bed in my cell, too weak to get up, several of the sisters arrived. They looked at me with sympathy and guilt as they handed me a box.

I looked questioningly at them. None of them returned my gaze. I slowly and carefully opened the box. It contained piles and piles of unopened mail addressed to me and written in the hand of my beloved Rose.

A fury raged within me but was soon quelled by a fit of coughing that sapped me of the strength to scream. Instead, I settled for one word. "Why?" I asked.

"You needed to be stopped," said one of the sisters. "It was not right. We belong only to God. It is not right for a bride of Christ to worship someone else so fiercely," she said with conviction.

"It is not right for a bride of Christ to interfere with the will of God," I replied with even more conviction. I lay back onto my pillow, my broken heart evident to all of them.

The sisters were horrified as they considered my words and finally recognised the full extent of their betrayal.

Against the orders of new Mother, they sent for my Rose to return to me, and several days later, she arrived. So grown up now, but still my sweet, sweet Rose.

"I feel so ashamed!" she cried at my bedside. "I'm so sorry. I should have known. I should have come. When you stopped writing, I thought you were mad at me. I wrote and I wrote, and I thought you had given up on me."

"It's all right, my darling. It's all OK. I would never give up on you."

The sisters shamefacedly told her about the letters. She too was furious, but when she turned back to me, there was only love in her eyes.

"You have always been and always will be my mother," she said, "and I'm just so happy that I am here to see you again."

"And you, my sweet Rose, have always been my daughter. I pray that one day God will reunite us that we may spend another lifetime together as family."

She gripped my hand and squeezed it. "I pray for that with all of my heart," she replied.

We joined our prayers together to make them strong.

That night, I heard the abbey bells ringing as God called me home. I smiled, content that, through all the hardship, I had done his work.

Out in the garden, they buried me with a small wooden cross and lovingly laid flowers. My beautiful Rose, with her coppery hair, fell to her knees and wept.

Epilogue

I put my pen down, satisfied that I had given my life story some substance. I remembered this old me so clearly, and now I felt that she had finally been heard.

I said a little prayer to God, thanking him for giving me this new life. For blessing me with wonderful parents who are still with me, for my brothers and sister, for my loving husband (and his family), and for my wonderful children, including my little Rose.

I thanked him for all of these good things as the ever-present reminder that the prayers of his children are always heard and answered.

About Guided

On the face of it, this is a simple story. The story of a girl and her search for safety, belonging, and ultimately, a better life. However, within the text is a more complex and multilayered story.

The main character, our lead, remains nameless, as do most of the other characters in the book. This is both purposeful and symbolic. As with much of history, the everyday people often become forgotten. The main character in this story is one such character. Pulled out of obscurity, her story is shared just in the way that each and every one of us has a story to share.

She plays the lead, but we are reminded that each and every character, though only mentioned briefly, also has his or her own story, if only someone would take the time to hear it or imagine it.

In our lead's world that is bleak and filled with nameless people, Rose becomes even more significant. In the main character's mind, Rose is the only thing worth naming.

It is interesting that, when our lead heads off into the turmoil of the world, she is only ten or eleven. She is still a child, yet she acts with a maturity that we can only aspire to today. She lives her life with dignity and moral fortitude, and though she never complains that her life was taken away at such a young age, she fights fiercely to protect her Rose from a similar fate at a similar age.

The story takes place in no clearly established country or setting, except to say that there are farms and rivers and hills. The setting is purposely unidentified, consistent with the theme that this could be anyone, anywhere, and to not distract us from the important issue, which is the experience.

The story progresses simply, and in places, we skip several years at a time. This mimics the effects of time on our memories, where we do not remember every detail in linear order but instead get a series of key moments or feelings that shape our understanding of ourselves and our past. If you think back on your life so far, what are some of the key moments that stand out for you?

Everywhere she goes, our lead manages to make meaningful connections and contributes to her environment. She looks up to her parents, the woman of the crowded house, and Mother Superior. Each of these characters has different strengths. Her parents were strong and loving and protective. The woman in the crowded house was clear and firm and kind.

Mother Superior represented her longest association and was someone stable and consistent in our lead's life. She was someone wise and balanced who understood the ways of the world and reflected on her actions prior to taking them. She respected the life and duties and responsibilities that were upon her, and she had such a strong belief in a higher power that she was able to prepare for the most surprising event of a baby's arrival with a calm matter-of-factness. Has there ever been a time in your life when you were this calm and centred? Do you have anyone in your life with these characteristics? How do they make you feel?

The key trait that was shared by her parents, the woman in the crowded house, and Mother Superior was their protectiveness. All of these characters stood up for those in their care, and her parents and the woman in the crowded house paid for this with their lives. It is both symbolic and powerful that her mother continued to protect her from beyond the grave. Do you believe that this was a worthy sacrifice? When have you ferociously protected someone, what happened?

There is a strong theme of loss in the book with our lead ultimately losing everyone and everything that had meaning to her.

The death of Mother Superior seems to come out of the blue—a turn of the page, and suddenly she is gone. There is no hint or no lead-up that it is about to happen, and this reflects the way our lead experienced it. The news of her parents' death was equally as shocking for her.

Throughout the story, we see the strength of all the characters. But in particular, we feel the connection among our lead's mother, who falls to her knees and weeps at the loss of her children; our lead, who falls to her knees and weeps over the loss of her family; and Rose, who falls to her knees and weeps over the death of her mother. The story seems to indicate to us that Rose, like the strong women who came before her, would compose herself and keep putting one foot in front of the other.

When our lead dies, we are led to question whether her strength has finally run out, as it appears that she gave up the will to live prior to her illness. Does this mean that she chose to become a victim or a martyr? When it says she gave in and her body collapsed, we get the feeling that she had some control over the illness that eventually consumed her.

Our lead experienced great shame about dreaming of a better life. After all, she had made the greatest possible commitment to God and his church and she should have been content with the life that he had afforded her. But she wanted more, and it wracked her with guilt.

At the time, she could not leave, and it made her angry with herself that she might even want to. She felt enraged at the sisters and new Mother for their cruelty, and internally she fought between wanting to forgive as her God would have her do and wanting to curse them all into the depths of hell. This brought forth more shame and more questioning as to whether they were right about her being the Devil's child and whether this bitterness and hatred confirmed that she actually was a wicked, evil person.

So she internalised it all. She carried this shame around with her like her own cross to bear.

The story brings us to question who the real enemies are. Are they the soldiers or those that are closest to us? Sometimes, the real terrorism occurs in our own homes in the places that are supposed to be the safest. We might even question whether she would have been better off with the children of the crowded house with an unknown fate.

Our lead was stuck in a situation that she could not readily walk away from, yet we are left to wonder this: What if she did have had the courage to walk away with Rose and to start a new life? What if she had the courage to stand up and say, "No more," to her tormentors?

We are also led to ponder where, in our own lives, we are similarly stuck. Through obligation, politeness, or other self-imposed imaginary restrictions, what would happen if we had the courage to walk away and start a fresh?

Our lead had to wait for a new life for this to happen, but we are not so restricted. We have opportunities that our lead did not have.

She felt ashamed to ask for a better life. Are you? She felt that she did not deserve it. How about you?

Our lead put up with this poor treatment during her time in the abbey; however, her action when Rose was being bullied was decisive and swift. What do you think held her back from standing up for herself and protecting herself from further attacks? In her position, how would you have acted or reacted? How successful was her action in regards to

Rose's situation? If you were in Rose's situation, how would you feel about our lead's actions?

Initially, when our lead met the soldiers with their dogs, she did not see them as enemies. When they returned the second time around, it is clear that the war has changed them. When she states, "They did not have the dogs this time. They did not need them," she is intimating that the soldiers had become the dogs—vicious and snarling. She is making us aware that a terrible experience like war has the power to turn normal people into savage enemies.

Through all of the negative experiences, however, our lead always holds firmly to her faith and uses her own talents.

Our lead had a gift or talent in being able to communicate with her angels and translating this experience into the written word. It is not something that she questions, and through Mother Superior, she finds a safe place to express her visions. In our lives, we all have talents and abilities, yet we often do not recognise our own greatness. What talents do you have that you have not recognised because they come so naturally? How could you begin to develop these talents?

Our lead sacrificed the opportunity for a better life, yet she did not see it this way. She found meaning in what she was doing, and this represents the beauty of the human spirit, accepting what she couldn't change and giving her all for what she believed in.

In many ways, Rose was her reward for persisting in life. We all have different currencies or things of value, and these differ depending on our life experiences. What is your currency? Is it money, love, respect, or material objects? How might this be different if you were in our lead's position?

As our lead's health deteriorates, she doesn't regret how her life turned out, but she begins to dream of a better life with a loving family. She shows us in that moment all of the things that she values above all else.

In the epilogue, we are led to believe that God answered her prayers and she was indeed reborn with all of the things that she wanted so much. What do you imagine that she will do with this lifetime? How much, and in what ways, do you think that she will be influenced by her previous life?

This story is a simple one but with much to ponder and reflect on. So on that note, here is one final thought: what if you and your life are actually the result of an answered prayer?